CHILDREN' SONGS

Midi Piano Library

Exclusive Distributors:

Music Sales Limited
8/9 Frith Street,
London W1V 5TZ, England.

Music Sales Pty Limited
120 Rothschild Avenue,
Rosebery, NSW 2018,
Australia.

Order No.AM91756
ISBN 0-7119-3875-X
This book © Copyright 1994 by Wise Publications

Book & pack design by 4i Limited
Arrangements by Paul Lawley
Music processed by Interactive Sciences Limited

Printed in the United Kingdom by
Caligraving Limited, Thetford, Norfolk.

Photographs courtesy of:
London Features International

Your Guarantee of Quality

As publishers, we strive to produce every book to the highest commercial standards.
The music has been freshly engraved and this book has been carefully designed to minimise awkward
page turns and to make playing from it a real pleasure. Throughout, the printing and binding have
been planned to ensure a sturdy, attractive publication which should give years of enjoyment. If your
copy fails to meet our high standards, please inform us and we will gladly replace it.

Music Sales' complete catalogue describes thousands of titles and is available in full colour sections
by subject, direct from Music Sales Limited. Please state your areas of interest and send a
cheque/postal order for £1.50 for postage to: Music Sales Limited, Newmarket Road,
Bury St. Edmunds, Suffolk IP33 3YB.

PREFACE

Included with this book you will find a brand new kind of music data disk. On this 3.5" disk
are digitally recorded Standard Midi Files (SMF). These files or songs can be played on any
dedicated or Computer based Standard Midi File player which conforms to the General MIDI
system (GM).

The files contain professionally recorded piano accompaniments plus full backing orchestration.
You can either listen to, or play along with the accompaniment. The right-hand of the piano is
on Midi Channel 4 and the left-hand on Midi Channel 3. According to the instructions for your
particular player you can mute the relevant channel and then practise each hand separately.

PREFACE

Ce livre est accompagné d'une disquette de données musicales d'un style tout nouveau.
En effet, cette disquette de 3,5" contient des fichiers MIDI standards (Standard MIDI Files,
ou SMF) enregistrés par procédé numérique. Ces fichiers, ou morceaux, peuvent être lus
par n'importe quel lecteur SFM dédié ou informatisé se conformant aux normes MIDI.

Les fichiers comprennent une mélodie au piano et un accompagnement orchestral de haute
qualité pour chacun des morceaux. Vous pouvez simplement écouter ces derniers, ou bien
jouer en même temps. Le piano est réparti entre les deux canaux MIDI – la main droite sur
le canal 4 et la main gauche sur le canal 3. Vous pouvez donc couper l'un des deux canaux
(en suivant les instructions pour votre machine) afin d'exercer chaque main séparément.

VORWORT

Diesem Notenbuch ist eine völlig neue Art von Musikdaten-Diskette beigelegt. Die 3,5" Diskette
enthält digital aufgezeichnete Standard MIDI Files (SMF), die dem General MIDI (GM)-System
entsprechen. Diese Files oder Musiktitel können auf jedem Sequenzer, der in der Lage ist,
SMF-Daten zu lesen, abgespielt werden.

Die einzelnen Musiktitel enthalten zum Klavier-Part eine professionell arrangierte Begleitung.
Sie können sich diese Musik anhören oder selbst zu den Arrangements spielen. Die Noten für
die rechte Hand des Klavier-Parts sind auf MIDI Kanal 4, die für den Part der linken Hand auf
MIDI-Kanal 3 aufgezeichnet.

Bitte beachten Sie die Bedienhinweise zu Ihrem Sequenzer, um den MIDI-Kanal oder die
entsprechende Spur stumm zu schalten, damit Sie die rechte und linke Hand separat zur
Begleitung spielen können.

PREFACIO

Incluido en este libro vd. encontrará un tipo completamente nuevo de disco de datos musicales.
En este disco de 3.5" hay Standard Midi Files (SMF) grabados digitalmente. Estos ficheros o
canciones pueden ser reproducidos en cualquier reproductor de Standard Midi Files diseñado
para allo o basado en ordenador que so ajuste al sistema General MIDI (GM).

Los ficheros contienen acompañamientos de piano grabados profesionalmente adamás de una
completa orquestación. Vd. puede o bien escuchar o bien tocar junto con el acompañamiento.
La mano derecha del piano está en Canal Midi 4 y la mano izquierda en Canal Midi 3.
De acuerdo con las instrucciones de su reproductor particular Vd. puede enmudecer el canal
oportuno y practicar cada mano separadamente.

PREMESSA

Incluso in questo libro. troverete un nuovo tipo di dati musicali su disco. In questo dischetto da
3,5" sono memorizzati Standard Midi File (SMF). Questi file o canzoni possono essere riprodotti
su qualsiasi lettore dedicato o computerizzato in grado di riconoscere gli Standard Midi File
conformi allle specifiche del sistema General Midi (GM).

I file contengono registrazioni professionali di accompagnamento di pianoforte complete di
orchestrazione strumentale. E' possibile suonare insieme alla parte di accompagnamento
o anche semplicemente ascoltare il brano. La parte della mano destra per pianoforte è
memorizzata sul Canale Midi 4, quella della mano sinistra sul Canale Midi 3. A seconda
dell'esigenza del singolo esecutore e possibile ammutolire (mute) il rispettivo canale delle
due parti e esercitare separatamente mano destra e mano sinistra.

Baa! Baa! Black Sheep

Traditional

Going To The Zoo

Words and Music by Tom Paxton

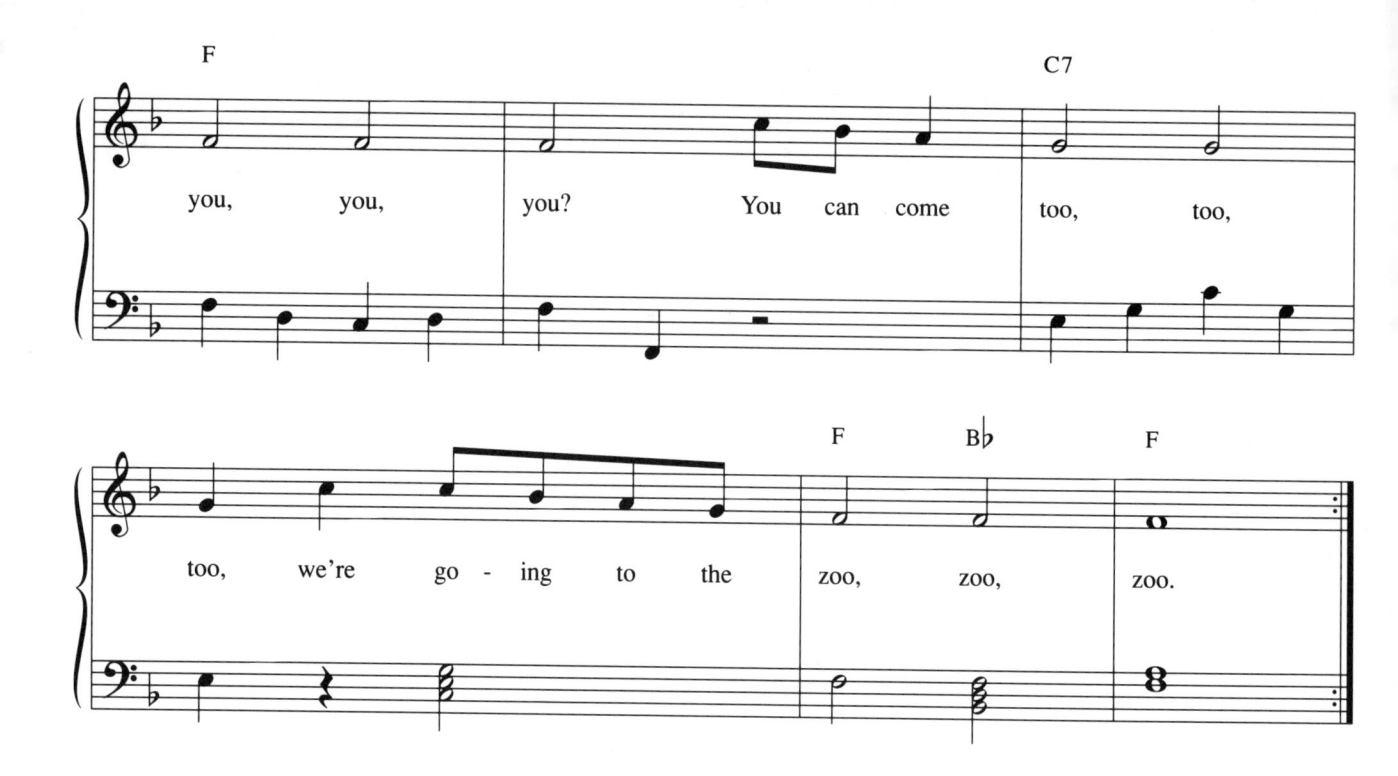

3. See all the monkeys scritch, scritch, scratchin',
   Jumpin' all around and scritch, scritch, scratchin',
   Hangin' by their long tails scritch, scritch, scratchin',
   We can stay all day.
   (*Chorus*)

4. Seals in the pool all honk, honk, honkin',
   Catchin' fish and honk, honk, honkin',
   Little seals honk, honk, honkin', (*high pitched voice*)
   We can stay all day.
   (*Chorus*)

5. (*Slower Tempo*)
   We stayed all day and I'm gettin' sleepy,
   Sittin' in the car gettin' sleep, sleep, sleepy,
   Home already and I'm sleep, sleep, sleepy,
   We have stayed all day.

   Chorus:
   We've been to the zoo, zoo, zoo,
   So have you, you, you,
   You came too, too, too,
   We've been to the zoo, zoo, zoo.

Nellie The Elephant

Words by Ralph Butler
Music by Peter Hart

11

Mary Had A Little Lamb

Traditional

3. It followed her to school one day,
   School one day, school one day,
   It followed her to school one day,
   Which was against the rule.

4. It made the children laugh and play,
   Laugh and play, laugh and play,
   It made the children laugh and play
   To see a lamb at school.

5. And so the teacher turned it out,
   Turned it out, turned it out,
   And so the teacher turned it out
   But still it lingered near.

6. And waited patiently about,
   'Ly about, 'ly about,
   And waited patiently about
   'Till Mary did appear.

7. Why does the lamb love Mary so?
   Mary so, Mary so,
   Why does the lamb love Mary so?
   The eager children cry.

8. Why Mary loves the lamb, you know,
   Lamb, you know, lamb, you know,
   Why Mary loves the lamb, you know,
   The teacher did reply.

Ob-La-Di, Ob-La-Da

Words and Music by John Lennon & Paul McCartney

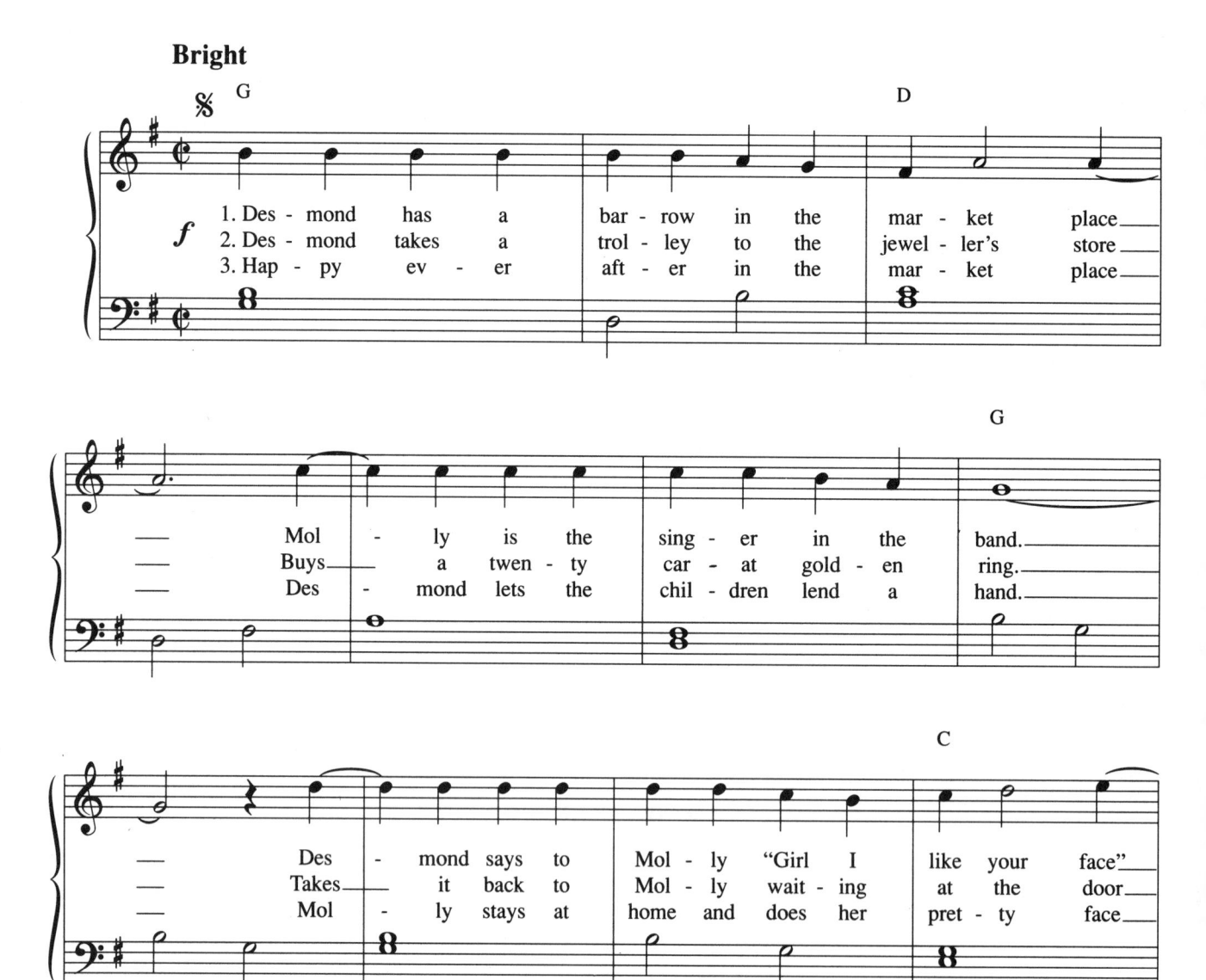

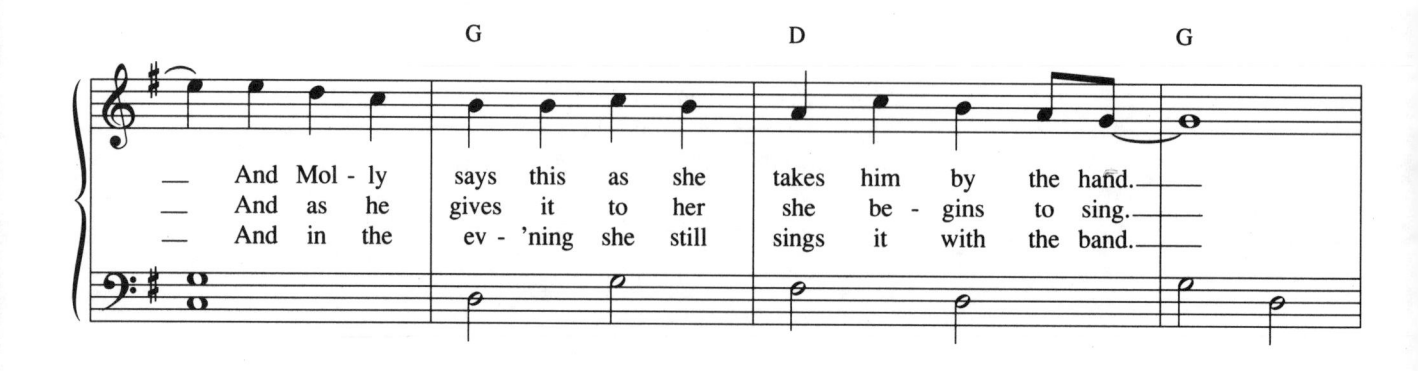

Three Blind Mice

Traditional

Old MacDonald Had A Farm

Traditional

Old MacDonald had a farm,
E - I - E - I - O.
And on that farm he had some ducks,
E - I - E - I - O.
With a quack-quack here, and a quack-quack there,
Here a quack, there a quack, everywhere a quack-quack,
Chick-chick here, and a chick-chick there,
Here a chick, there a chick, everywhere a chick-chick.
Old MacDonald had a farm,
E - I - E - I - O.

. . . And on that farm he had some cows . . .
With a moo-moo here, and a moo-moo there,
Here a moo, there a moo, everywhere a moo-moo,
Quack-quack here and a quack-quack there . . .
Chick-chick here and a chick-chick there . . .

. . . And on that farm he had some pigs . . .
With an oink-oink here, and an oink-oink there . . .
A moo-moo here . . .
Quack-quack here . . .
Chick-chick here . . .

. . . And on that farm he had some sheep . . .
With a baa-baa here, and a baa-baa there . . .

Pop Goes The Weasel

Traditional

Gaily

1. All a-round the cob-bler's bench The mon-key chased the wea-sel, The mon-key thought 'twas all in fun. Pop! goes the wea-sel. A pen-ny for a spool of thread, A pen-ny for a nee-dle, That's the way the mo-ney goes Pop! goes the wea-sel.

2. John-ny Bull he makes his brag To whip the whole cre-a-tion. Why don't he take Se-bas-to-pol. Pop! goes the wea-sel. Queen Vic-to-ria's ve-ry sick, Na-po-leon's got the mea-sles, Se-bas-to-pol's not tak-en yet. Pop! goes the wea-sel.

3. May - or Wood's put the rum sel - lers through The Maine law's sad and ev - il. We can - not get our tod - dy now, Pop! goes the wea - sel. The but - cher when he char - ges for meat, sticks in the bone and gris - tle. But that's the way the mon - ey goes. Pop! goes the wea - sel.

Puff (The Magic Dragon)

Words and Music by Peter Yarrow & Leonard Lipton

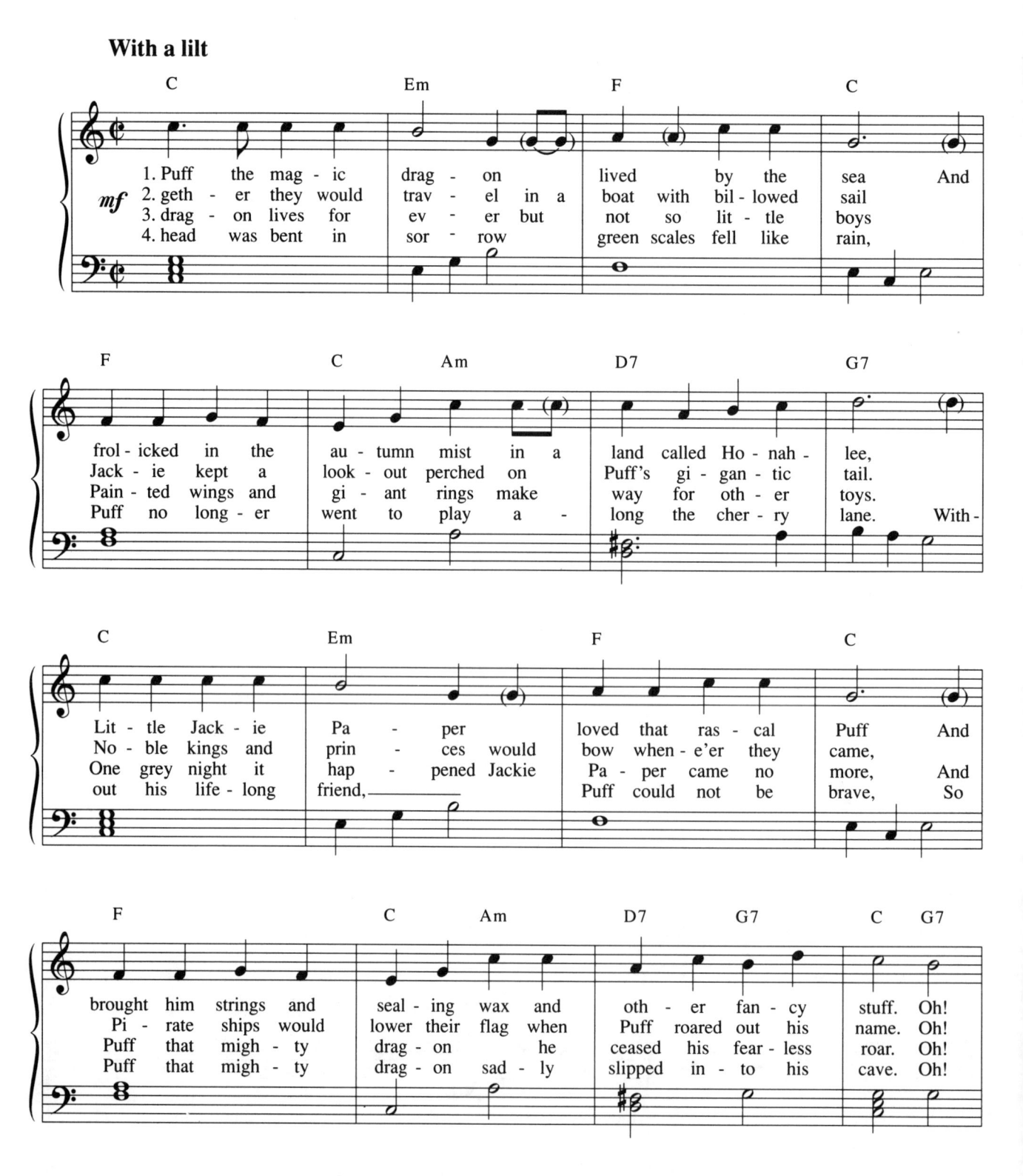

Three Wheels On My Wagon

Words by Bob Hilliard
Music by Burt Bacharach

Moderately

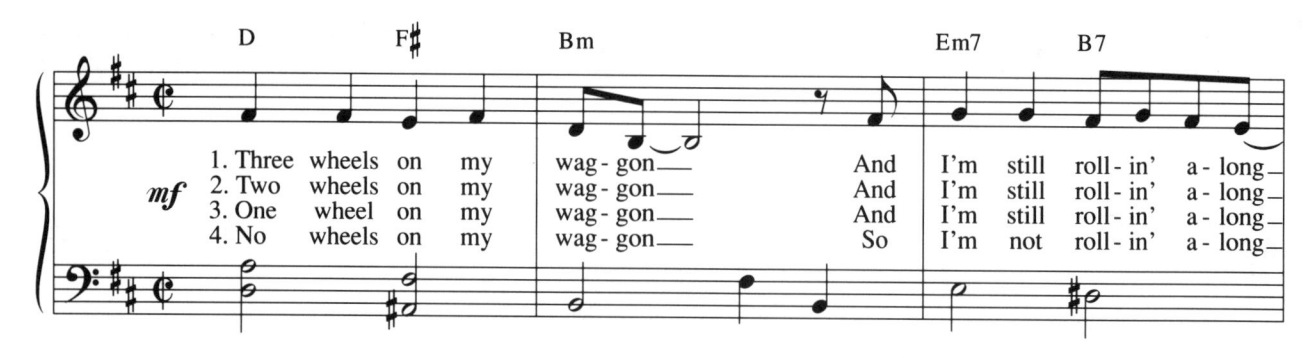

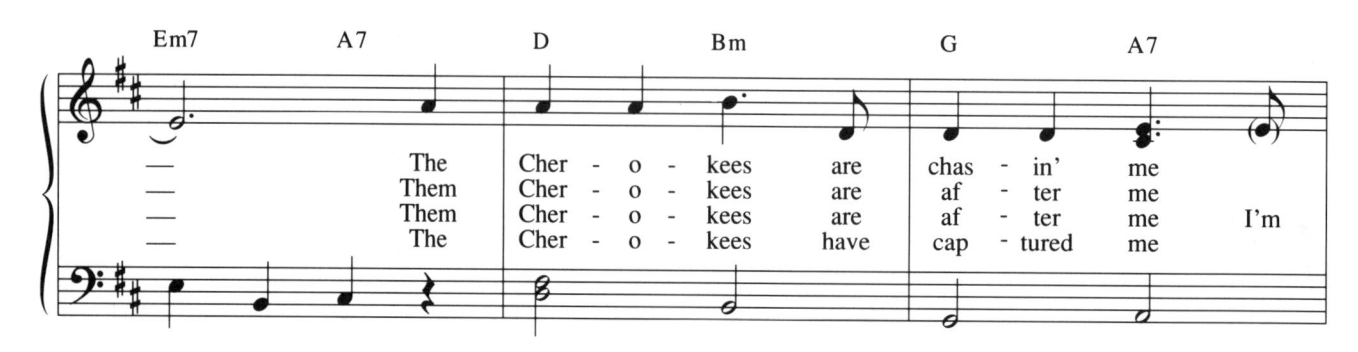

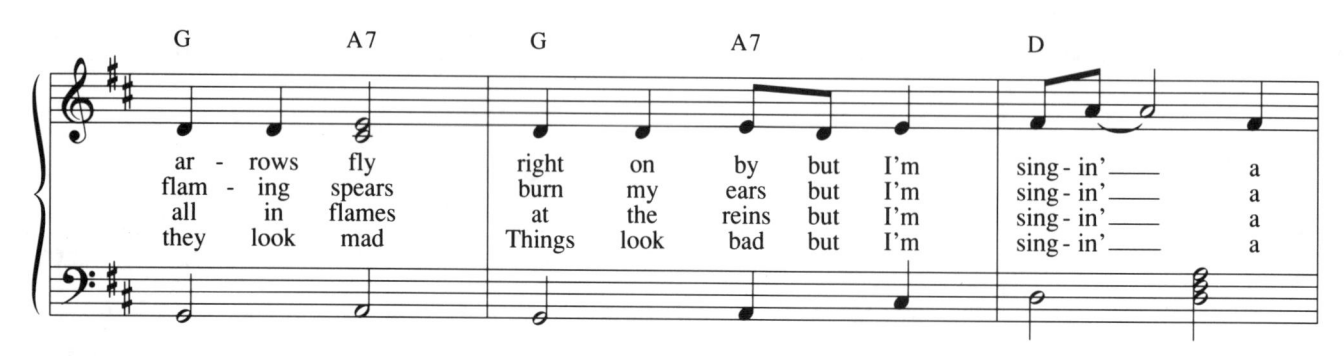

(Spoken) *Come on all you Cherokees, sing along with me*

When You Come To The End Of A Lollipop

Words and Music by Al Hoffman & Dick Manning

Moderately

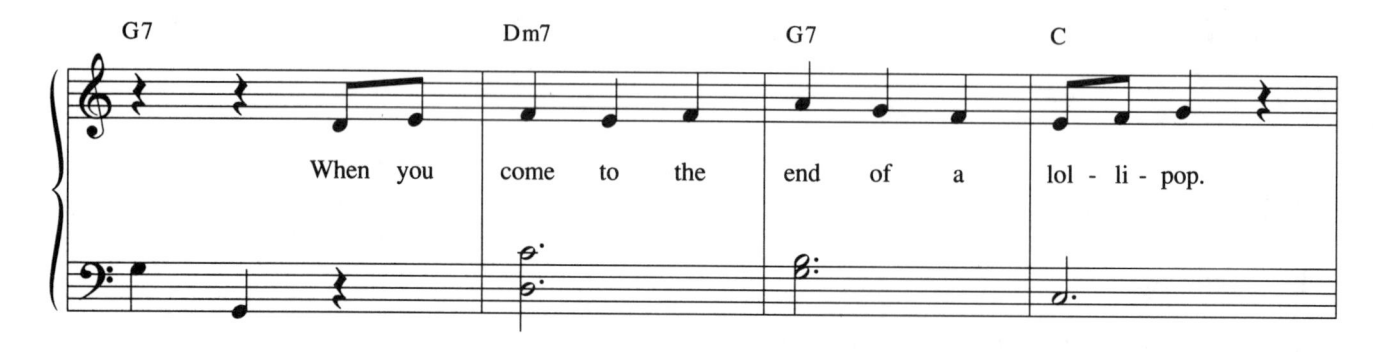

Gil - ly - o, Gil - ly - o, I love my

lol - ly - o! 1. Down to the ve - ry last lick.
2. Win - ter and sum - mer and spring.

But what can you do with it when you are
But when you are done it's a - bout as much

thro' with it? All you have left is the stick!
fun as a yo - yo with - out an - y string!

When you

CODA

heart.

29

You're A Pink Toothbrush

Words and Music by Ralph Ruvin, Bob Halfin & Harold Irving